BEDTIME SLEEP MEDITATIONS FOR KIDS

Short Stories with Positive Affirmations to Help Children & Toddlers Fall Asleep at Night, Relax, And Have Beautiful Dreams (Book 1)

Author: Sleepy Willow

Copyright 2021 – All rights reserved.

The content contained within this book may not be reproduced, duplicated or transmitted without direct written permission from the author or the publisher.

Under no circumstances will any blame or legal responsibility be held against the publisher, or author, for any damages, reparation, or monetary loss due to the information contained within this book. Either directly or indirectly.

Legal Notice:

This book is copyright protected.

This book is only for personal use. You cannot amend, distribute, sell, use, quote or paraphrase any part, or content within this book, without the consent of the author or publisher.

Disclaimer Notice:

Please not the information contained within this document is for educational and entertainment purposes only.

No warranties of any kind are declared or implied. Readers acknowledge that the author is not engaging in the rendering of legal, financial, medical or professional advice.

The content within this book has been derived from various sources. Please consult a licensed professional before attempting any techniques outlined in this book.

By reading this document, the reader agrees that under no circumstances is the author responsible for any losses, direct or indirect, which are incurred as a result of the use of the information contained within this document, including, but not limited to: errors, omissions, or inaccuracies.

Table of content

Introduction 1

Chapter 1 3
   Your Perfect Paradise 3

Chapter 2 22
   The Land Of Unicorns 22

Chapter 3 40
   Lovely Ocean Adventures 40

Chapter 4 73
   Magical Forest Friends 73

Chapter 5 98
   Positive Bedtime Affirmations 98

Conclusion 111

INTRODUCTION

Thank you for choosing *Bedtime Meditations For Kids Book 1*.

In this magical and wonderful book, you will be taken on many adventures and listen to wonderful stories that will help you to fall asleep peacefully every night. I hope that you and your children will have hours of fun reading these stories. Each story in this book will be entertaining and will have small lessons that your child can learn from. You will learn many skills that can help you relax your mind and body, so you have the most amazing sleep every night. Each story contains valuable lessons while relieving stress. Each story will empower you and your children to improve your self-confidence and self-esteem. You will learn how to deal with your emotions better and communicate them more effectively.

Children who experience lots of nightmares might be scared to fall asleep at night and might have a hard time relaxing at night because they are afraid of scary dreams. This book will help you combat and get rid of those fears. Each story will help you feel more relax, calm, loved and completely safe. You have nothing to worry about from now on.

After you have brushed your teeth, combed your hair and put on nice comfortable pajamas, it's time for you to snuggle down in bed and get ready for sleep. You can now pick any story to help you relax and drift off to an amazing sleep.

Make sure you read each story and follow along. Each story has a relaxing meditation to help you get cozy and comfortable for a good night's sleep.

Are you ready to begin your bedtime meditation stories? Choose any story to begin your adventure now!

CHAPTER 1

Your Perfect Paradise

Close your eyes and take a nice deep breath.
Allow your tummy to fill up like a balloon.
Then slowly exhale gently and smoothly.

Take another deep breath,
allowing your tummy to fill up like a balloon.
And slowly and gently exhale.
One more time take a nice big deep breath,
Allowing your tummy to fill up like a balloon.
The slowly and gently exhale,
And relax.

Now, imagine yourself in your bedroom.
You notice something is glimmering and shining on your bedroom wall.
You can see what it is,

And you are not scared of it at all.
In fact, you are drawn towards it,
and you feel quite excited.
As you begin to take a closer look at it,
It appears to be pulsing and shimmering like a thousand stars.
It seems to be some kind of portal into another world.

You extend and dip your hand in the portal and does not hurt at all.
In fact, it feels really nice.
It feels warm and soothing to the touch.
Can you feel it?
Now dip your head in and take a little peak on the other side.
Wow!
This is truly amazing!
It's is a portal to paradise.
In this paradise you can see all of your favorite things.
You can see theme parks, water parks, and you can even see flying unicorns.
What else can you see with all of your favorite things?

Now you fully walk through this portal, and you instantly feel happy.
You feel full of joy.
This paradise doesn't just have all of your favorite things,
But it also makes you feel amazing on the inside too.
A place where you can leave any worries and stresses behind you.
In this place, well you just feel happy.

You notice a welcome banner with your name on it.
This place is just for you.
You can invite anyone you want to it.
Spend some time now in your very own paradise.
Maybe you can take a ride on a unicorn.
Maybe you can play with fairies.
Maybe you can even take a ride on a waterslide.
You may even want to see a special person or a pet that you can no longer see in your normal life.
You decide this is your special place

In this place, it not only allows you to be around all of your favorite things,
It also allows you to see only the good and beauty in all things.

Even with the people you don't usually like.
Here you can see only the good in them.
You can see only the goodness all around you.
You can see the good and beauty in every situation.
Badness has no place here.
You can see the beauty in everything.
You can feel the beauty in everything.
Even the things you think are ordinary in everyday life like the leaves of a tree, or like the grass under your bare feet.
Can you see it?

Can you feel it?

It's now time to come back from this beautiful place.
So, you jump through the portal and return back to your room.
But you have now brought back with you all those feelings of joy and happiness.
Best of all you can return back to your portal of paradise whenever you like.

Now imagine you are walking towards the ocean.
Walking through a beautiful tropical forest.

You can see the trees around you are very tall, very elegant.
You can even smell the fresh clean air.
You can hear the sounds of all the different animals and birds in this forest.
Can you hear them?

You start to hear the waves from the ocean ahead of you.
You can hear the sound of them coming up under the sand on the beach.
You can even smell the ocean spray.
The lovely smell that you can only find at the beach.
Can you smell it?
You continue to walk along your path getting closer to the sea.
As you come to the edge of the trees,
You see the brilliant blue color of the ocean ahead.

You can hear the magnificent sound of the ocean waves.
They are so much louder now.
You walk out of the forest and onto a long stretch of glorious white sand.

The sand is very soft as you take off your shoes and your socks.
You walk through the warm white Sun rays towards the water.
You can feel the Sun beneath your feet and start to feel it between your toes.
Can you feel it?

This beach is very wide and very long.
It stretches for miles ahead.
You can hear the waves washing up onto the shore.
You can smell the colleen saltwater.
You can even smell the clean crisp air.
You look again at the ocean and it is the deepest and most beautiful blue you have ever seen.

Now imagine yourself walking toward the water.
Under the fine hot Sun, you're feeling a little hot now.
Just a little bit sticky too.
As you walk, you can see the sparkles of the sunshine dance upon the water's surface.
It's like a million tiny stars all shining and dancing just for you.
It looks so beautiful.

A wave washes over the Sun towards you and you can feel it touch your toes before gently receding.
As you step forward more waves wash over your feet.
It feels so cool and refreshing.
It is so calming and soothing on your feet.
You begin to walk a bit further into the clear clean water.
You can see the white foam under the water.
You can still feel the water between your toes.
Can you feel your toes squashed into the sand and wriggling them about in the water?

You can now see a few small fish swimming.
Fast positive flashes of color as they pass by.
The water is very pleasant and cool, but not too cold.
You walk a little further into the water,
And you decide you want to take a gentle swim.
So, enjoy the ocean for a few minutes.
Allow yourself to float and drift around in the beautiful deep blue ocean.
Just float around with all the little fish
And just relax.

Now, you are feeling very calm and refreshed.
You're feeling very peaceful and very very relaxed.
You walk out of the water and back onto the beach again.
Feeling again the soft sand beneath your feet and your toes.
You walk along the water's edge and you feel free of any worries you might have had.
All of your problems have been washed away,
And now you only feel very calm, very peaceful and so relaxed.
You turn around and you see a comfortable lounge chair and a towel just for you.
You go over and sit on the chair.
You like sitting on the chair and maybe
You may decide to spread the towel in the Sun and just relax on the chair.
Just relaxing and enjoying the sunshine and
The cool breeze upon your face.
The warmth of the sun on your skin.
The sound of the waves making you feel every so peaceful.
Making you fel every so happy just watching the waves
Rise and flow.
Backwards and forwards.
Backwards and forwards.

You feel so calm.
So calm so relaxed and very very peaceful.
You just sit there for a little while longer.
Enjoying the lovely relaxation that has been made just for you.

Now, it's time for you to return back to your normal life.
It's time to come back home now.
Imagine you're standing on a beach.
On your very own private magical island.
A place that's yours.
A place where you can relax and feel very safe.
This magical island of yours is surrounded by the bluest ocean.
The water sparkles and shines like a thousand diamonds glittering in the Sun.
Above your island is a rainbow of many colors.
Can you see it floating above your island?
Can you see it in the sky?

You turn and look into the distance and you see the tops of mountains.
Some of them reaching so high you can see snow on the very tips of them.

You start walking towards the amazing forest and to the pathway that will lead you to these beautiful mountains.
You step onto the path and begin to walk.
You can hear birds singing.
Can you hear them?
You can see many flowers blooming in many colors.
You can hear the sounds of tiny animals rustling in the bushes as they go about their day.
You can't see them but you can hear them
Listen

Your pathway starts to rise now.
You can feel the muscles in your legs getting tighter as you walk.
Your heart begins to beat just a little bit faster.
Up ahead of you, you see an animal waiting for you.
It's your guide for the rest of your journey.
What animal can you see?
It is your favorite animal?
Or is it one you haven't seen before?
Your animal guide beckons for you to follow it.
So you do and the two of you walk in a very blissful silence.
So peaceful you think how nice it is to be with a friend.

A friend where it's ok if you don't talk.
It's okay just to be together happily walking along.
You can hear the birds singing their songs as they fly high above you.
You and your animal guide stop for a little rest.
You see a bench and the two of you sit on it for a little while.
Your animal guide sits beside you saying nothing at all.
The two of you just sit in a peaceful silence.
You spend a few moments just sitting and being still and quiet with your animal guide.
Look around you and just enjoy how peaceful it is hear and just listen.

Your journey to the top of the peaceful mountain with your guide ends now.
Your guide points you in the direction you need to go with a single light showing you the way.
This part of the journey you walk alone but that's okay,
Because you don't mind.
You feel so safe, so peaceful and fell so well protected.
You begin to walk.

You reach the top and find a very old stone village on the edge of the mountain.
You can see an old bridge with a gentle waterfall flowing back down the mountainside.
There is a beautiful garden just outside of the village walls.
You see a small group of people sitting in a circle on the ground.
One of them turns and welcomes you, but not with their voice.
With their thoughts and beautiful smile.

You walk over to them and take your place beside them in a circle.
Thoughts pop into your head telling you that you're with a tribe of very peacefull people.
People who don't talk.
They don't use their voices.
They are all wearing white robes
And they give you one to put on.
You feel like you've been here before.
It feels like home to you.
It's so peaceful here.
You have never felt so at peace.
You know in your heart that just by being you will never feela lone again.

These are the people of silence.
Their language is silence.
You don't even have to hear their thoughts.
You just know what they are telling you.
You can feel it through the silence.
You learn so much more truth than anything else because
you can feel the truth in your heart.
This really makes your soul sing with happiness and peace.
You look around and see beautiful vistas all around the top of the mountain.
You really do know that you will never be alone again.
You finally realize that everything is perfect just the way it is,
as you sit there atop the mountain.
You feel so big,
You feel so connected and apart of everything.
You feel as one with the world and with these people of silence.
You realize that all of the answers to your questions can be found in this beautiful silence.
Its makes you feels so at peace.
You also know that the only time these wonderful beings use their voices is when they sing.
When they sing it's like angels are talking to you.

These beautiful people of silence know that to sing is to connect to your heart.
The people of silence begin to sing.

Can you hear it?

Can you feel it?

You have never heard anything like it before.
These words touch your heart in a way that you have never felt before.
It really does make your soul sing with complete and utter joy.
Listen even closer.
What can you hear?

What can you feel with your soul?
You become totally immersed in this beautiful song.
It's almost like a soulful lullaby tempting you to sleep.

So, sit for a little while in silence with these amazing people.
Just listen.
Lay your head on the soft and gentle grass.

If sleep comes calling just listen and remember.
You can return any time you wish,
and spend time with the people of silence and just listen.

Now imagine there is a tiny door in the back of your mind.
On that door there is a sign and it says sleeping mind.
Can you see it?
Can you see the sign?
You open the door and enter the most beautiful bedroom.
This is your favorite room.
Inside this bedroom you can have anything you want.
All of your favorite things to help you relax and feel safe.
This is your room and it can be any way you want it to be.
Anything that makes you feel happy and relaxed.
You can have any kind of bed you want.
It can be a great big bed or it can be a bed that looks like a racing car.
It can be a bed that's surrounded with unicorns to help you sleep.

It can even be a bed that is just a cloud and it floats above your floor.
Anything you want you can have.
Even your favorite teddy bear or toy can be there with you.
This wonderful bed of yours can have the most amazing fluffy pillows for you to lay your head on, and the softest quilt to keep you warm and help you snuggle down.
This room is the perfect temperature for you, just the way you like it.
There is a lovely scent of lavender flowers drifting around the room.
You don't know where its coming from, but it smells lovely and relaxing.
The only sound you can hear is the perfect and gentle music.
It's very soft in the background.
So very peaceful.
You really like it as you listen to the sounds of the music.
You realize that nobody can disturb you in your peaceful place.
This peaceful place with your sleepy mind.
This is a place to let go all your thoughts.
All your worries because they don't matter here.
It's very safe and you will only ever feel happy and sleepy when you are here.

So, for a few moments create your perfect bedroom in your mind.
Create all the things that bring you peace.
Make it look just how you want it to be.

Now that you have the most perfect bedroom,
you climb upon your perfect bed.
You lay your head upon the soft and fluffy pillows.
You give a great big sigh of happiness.
You look over to the large window with beautiful curtains hanging on either side of it.
Through this window you can see the night sky,
and the beautiful stars shining like diamonds glittering so brightly.
You stare at them for a few minutes and imagine that you can see lots of other beds just floating high above you in the night sky.
Each of those beds has someone in them just like you all gently drifting off to sleep.
So now if you like, you can leave the curtains open and sleep by the light of the stars.
Or you can use your own mind and slowly close them and shut out the stars to get ready for sleep.
It's so peaceful, calm and quiet in your mind now.
Just enjoy it.

Your eyes are feeling really heavy now.
Your body is feeling so very tired.
You take a deep breath in through your nose and gently blow it out from your mouth.
You take another deep breath and gently blow it out from your mouth.
You're feeling very sleepy now.
So tired and relaxed.
You feel a gently wave of sleepiness starting at your feet.
It's a warm and gently feeling.
Kind of like how a feather feels when you brush it against your skin.
So soft and gently.
You can feel your toes going to sleep.
It feels warm and tingly ever so soft.
You feel the soothing gently wave of sleepiness going up your calves and your shins.
You can feel it going up your thighs.
You think your legs have already gone to sleep.
You feel very tired now.
So sleepy.
So happy.
It feels like you can't open your eyes, but that's okay.
You don't need to open your eyes.

This beautiful wave of sleepiness travels all the way up your body, down your arms and into your hands, making you body feel very very heavy.
Very very tired and very very sleepy.
This gently warm wave of sleepiness travels up your face and over the top of your head, down the back of your neck.
You feel so tired, so sleepy now.
You feel nice and warm and snuggly under the soft quilt and your very fluffy pillow.
Just have a little sleep now.
I am going to count from 5 to 1.
Remember the time we get to 1 you'll be asleep are you ready?

5
You feel so sleepy.
4
So tired for feeling warm and safe.
3
Feeling so protected.
2
Feeling so very very safe.
1

Feeling so very very loved.
Night night.
Sleep tight.

CHAPTER 2

The Land Of Unicorns

Close your eyes and make yourself comfortable.
Take a deep breath in through your nose.
The slowly and gently breathe out through your mouth.

Again, take another deep breath in through your nose.
Then slowly and gently breath through your mouth.
One more time, deep breath in.
And slowly and gently breathe out through your mouth.

Now bring your breathing back to its normal rhythm.
Feeling your chest rise and fall gently.

Feeling peaceful and calm.
Feeling very relaxed.
With each breath you take, you can feel yourself becoming more and more relaxed.
Your body feels quite floppy and you feel so peaceful now.
So relaxed and yet you feel very happy and very light.
Your breathing is almost still.
You are so relaxed.

Now, imagine yourself sitting in a large green field.
The sun is shining brightly and it's a very beautiful clear day.
You can see for miles and miles.
You feel very calm, very relaxed and ever so peaceful.
You can hear birds singing to each other.
Can you hear them?
As you look up at the sky, you see a beautiful rainbow of many colors.
The colors are so bright and so clear.
Can you see it?
Can you see how the colors sparkle and shine?
Can you see how the colors look almost alive?

You feel so drawn to this amazing rainbow that you walk towards it.
As you do, you feel your steps becoming lighter and lighter.
It's almost as if you are floating towards the rainbow.
It feels like your feet are not even touching the ground.

You stopped at the beginning of the rainbow.
You take a good look at it, and you realized the rainbow is actually moving.
It's actually a moving walkway.
Oh my goodness!
The rainbow stops moving and you step onto it.
As soon as you step onto it, the rainbow begins to move again.
As it moves forward it also begins to climb.
It climbs higher and higher.
You can even touch the colors of this rainbow.
What does it feel like to touch the rainbow?

The rainbow goes higher still.
You can now see the field below you.
You can see many trees.

You can see the birds flying.
There are even a couple of birds flying past your rainbow.
Can you see them?
The rainbow reaches the topmost part and begins to move back down again.
Now it's starting to get a bit slippy, so you sit down.
As you do, you begin to slide down.

Oh dear! You are sliding down the rainbow.
The rainbow is like a great big waterslide with beautiful colors all around you.
You are going faster and faster.
The wind is whipping through your hair making it fly everywhere.
This makes you laugh out loud.
You are laughing so hard that your tummy starts to hurt!

You can see the end of the rainbow and it's coming fast.
You notice that at the bottom of the rainbow, there appears to be a huge trampoline.
Oh my! You hit the trampoline so fast that you bounce right back up again.

Then back down, then right back up again.
This is so much fun!
So, you keep bouncing for a few minutes, up and down, up and down.

With each bounce, you see in the distance beautiful colors that you haven't seen before.
You can see many many fields and mountains.
You can see beautiful flowers too.
You've never seen them before either.
It's absolutely breathtaking to see such beauty.
You can also see what looks like horses in the distance, but they horns.
What cant be right.
Not unicorns surely no.
They can't be unicorns can they?
You stop bouncing and jump off the trampoline.
Go and investigate.
Go and see if they are really unicorns.
You start walking when you come across a huge sign and it says welcome to Unicornia, Land of The Unicorns.
Wow!
You look around you and you see unicorns everywhere!

There are large unicorns, there are small baby unicorns, there are unicorns all over the place!
Each and every one of them has a very special spiral horn on its head.
You move very quietly and very softly because you don't want to scare any of them away.
You don't want to frighten them.

You needn't worry because they are not scared of you at all.
In fact, they come up to you and say hello.
Yes, these beautiful and special beings couldn't talk.
They are very magical beings and they always know the truth og things.
The unicorns all speak at once.
They want to know your name.
They want to know how you got here, because only special good-hearted people can find the rainbow to Unicornia.

All of a sudden, the unicorns all stop talking and bow their heads.
A very different unicorn comes out from the rest of them.
This unicorn is very very beautiful.

She is much whiter than the others and her coat is very silky and very shiny.
She is a sparkling, glittering, magical unicorn and she looks about he same age as you.
You notice she has a diamond encrusted spiral horn with pink crystals on top of her head.
She has a beautiful silver mane with speckles of pink in it and beautiful silvers.
This magnificent unicorn walked so softly her hooves make no sounds.
Her spiral horn is the most powerful of them all.
Her spiral horn has the strongest healing qualities and it is magnificent.
The gentle breeze blows her across her spiral horn it produces a beautiful flute like melody.
It sounds so wonderful to you.
This unicorn is the princess of unicornia.
She is very special indeed.
She is a symbol of purity and grace.
She is such a powerful being and all she wants is for everyone to have peace and harmony in their life.

The princess unicorn speaks to you.
She tells you that magic is real.
She tells you that you must always believe in yourself,

and that you are so very special.
She is very gentle and loving, and you can feel the love she has for you.
She loves all beings.
She loves each and every one of us equally no matter how different we may look from each other.
She only sees the beautiful person we truly are.

The princess unicorn askes you if you would like to ride on her back.
Well of course you say yes.
She bows down for you to climb up, and when you are settled she starts to move.
For a few moments, you ride on the back of this majestic being.
Listen to what she has to tell you.
This magnificent place is unicornia.

The princess unicorn stops in front of these massive steps.
On these steps at the top, you see many beautiful crystals.
You climb down off her back.
She tells you to come up the steps with her.

As you walk up the steps you see that right in front of you is a beautiful crystal palace.
It shines and sparkles in the sunlight.
It is so beautiful and so magnificent.
The princess unicorn leads you up to the doors and two rather small elves open the doors.
You step inside and it is absolutely beautiful.
The princess unicorn asks if you like to around the palace and see how the live.
Would you like to see the princess's own bedroom?
You say "Oh yes please, this is wonderful."
The princess unicorn leads you up the great big stairs.
She is so excited she wants to take you to her bedroom first.
You go up with her and for a little while explore this beautiful palace.
You meet her family but most of all you see her bedroom.
What exciting things she has in there.
Just for a little while longer be in the palace.

Now it's time for you to return to your own home.
It's time for you to leave unicornia.
You thank the princess for all her kindness and for all that she has done for you today.

The princess tells you that you can come back here anytime you want.
There are many more things for you to visit.
There are many more beings for you to make friends with.
Before you go she asks you to touch her beautiful spiral horn.
As you do you feel a tiny shock.
It doesn't hurt. It just makes you jump a little.
You can feel a warm tingling sensation coming form her beautiful horn.
The princess unicorn tells you that she is sending her healing power to you.
Her healing power is in her beautiful spiral horn.
Any problems or worries that you may have had, is now being helped from the princess.
She is helping you overcome any difficulties that you may have.
She says she will be your best friend forever.
This makes you so happy you thank her for helping you.
You say goodbye.
You say goodbye to all the beautiful magical unicorns.
You turn to go.
The unicorn teaches us to believe in ourselves and in the reality of magic.

Remember those who don't believe in magic will never find it.
So, take a deep breath in.
Slowly and gently breathe out.
Deep breath in and slowly and gently breathe out.
One last time, deep breath in and slowly and gently breathe out.
Now, wiggle your fingers and wiggle your toes.
Slowly and gently open your eyes.

Find a place where you can sit, lay down, relax and not be disturbed.
Maybe in your bedroom or on your sofa.
Now, I want you to take a deep breath in through your nose.
And slowly and gently breathe out through your mouth again.
Deep breath in, and slowly and gently breathe out through your mouth.
One more time, deep breathe in and slowly and gently breathe out through your mouth.
Now just relax and let your breathing come back to its normal rhythm.

Now, I want you to imagine that you roots sprouting our from the soles of your feet.
Very strong, very noble roots.

They look like roots from a tree.
You can hear your roots growing through the ground.
You can hear them as they push their way through the soil.
Can you hear it?
Can you feel the soil under your feet all squishy?

Now imagine a beautiful white light surrounding your whole body.
A light so bright, that you shine brighter than a thousand suns.
It doesn't hurt you to look at it.
This beautiful white light is protecting you.

Now, imagine you are standing on your favorite beach.
A beach with golden sand.
You can feel the warm sun.

Sand beneath your bare feet and in between your toes.
Can you feel the sun tickling your feet?
Can you feel how warm it is?
Can you hear the sound of the ocean waves as they gently wash up on the sand?
You can even smell the salty air.
Can you smell it?
If you stick your tongue out, you can even taste it.
Try it.
Try and taste the salty air.
Stick your tongue out.
Can you taste it?

In the distance something catches your eye.
You squint your eyes to see what is moving towards you.
You are not afraid though because there is nothing here to be afraid of.
This is your special place and only you can say who comes to this place because it's yours.
You can now see what is coming towards you.
It is five unicorns.
Wow!
They stop in front of you and let you stroke them.

They are all truly beautiful creatures all soft and shiny.
Each unicorn is a different color.
Each of them have a gold and sparkling horn in the center of their head.
It glitters in the sunlight.
What colors are your unicorns? Can you feel their silky coats?

These are you own special unicorns that can take you on wonderful adventures.
With them you can co to far off lands.
You can see many different villages and see how other people live.
You can do to the desert if you want.
You can see the pyramids.
You can climb the highest mountain.
Where would you like to go?
What would you like to see?

One of the unicorns bows to their knees for you so that you can climb on their back.
You now climb up in its back.

It's your unicorn.
Male or female.
You wonder if they have a name, so you ask them.
You wait for them to whisper to you.
You unicorn asks where you want to go so you whisper it in their ear.

The unicorns all move as if they were one.
You hold on tight to the main as they start to trot.
You start to jiggle a bit as they move a bit quicker.
You feel very peaceful and calm on the back of your unicorn.
You feel excited and very happy.
You can feel the wind on your face.
You can feel the wind rushing through your hair.
You look up towards the sky and see the beautiful warm sun shining down on you.
It feels really lovely on your skin.

As your unicorn gallops forward have a look around you.
What do you see?

Do you see fields and trees?
Or do you see the ocean again?
What do you see?

You feels o happy riding on the back of your unicorn. So peaceful and free.

You notice that all five of the unicorns all move exactly at the same time.

They are never out of step with each other.

They are so I harmony with each other that when you unicorn, who is in the front, moves a just a tiny bit, they all move exactly the same way, at exactly the same time.

You see up ahead a cliff edge, and you wonder why your unicorns are not slowing down.

All of a sudden each one of them grows beautiful gold and silver wings.

As they keep galloping faster and faster, they rise into the air higher and higher.

They go soaring up into the clouds.

Do you realize that you are flying?

They are flying!

You feel so amazing, so joyful and so happy.

You are flying.

You look around you and you see fluffy white clouds everywhere.

You and your unicorns fly around for a while.

Doing all that you see, so be free and just fly with your unicorns.

Your unicorns start to dive downwards now back through the clouds.
You can feel the tremendous rush of air on your face.
You can feel your clothes blowing in the wind.
You look beneath you and see the glorious countryside below you.
What else do you see?
You and your unicorns are flying over the fields and hills.
Racing past tall trees swaying in the breeze.
You feel so happy.
You feel so alive.
How does it feel to be so free?

Keep flying for as long as you wish.
Maybe you can ask your unicorn a question.
Is there anything you would like to ask your unicorn?

Now it's time to return home.
Just whisper in your unicorn's ear and ask them to take you home.
Whenever you feel ready to open your eyes just wiggle your fingers and toes.

Have a big stretch and then slowly and gently open your eyes.

Close your eyes now and make yourself comfortable.
Take a deep breath in through your nose.
And slowly and gently breathe out through your mouth.
Take another deep breath in and slowly and gently breathe out.

CHAPTER 3

Lovely Ocean Adventures

Settle yourself down into your lovely cozy bed.
We'll begin now.
First tense up all of your muscles and hold it for a few seconds.
Hold it tightly and let go allowing your arms and legs to nice and limp.
Now breathe in deeply really filling up your lungs with air.
Really fill them up.
Now breathe out slowly and gently.
Releasing all the air from your lungs.
Now breathe in again slowly and deeply.
And hold your breath for just a moment.
Hold your breath.

And breathe out.

Draw in another deep breath.
Hold the breath.

And breathe out.
Breathe in.
And breathe out.
Breathe in.
And breathe out.
Every time you breathe in you become more and more relaxed.
You can feel your body becoming very loose, very soft.
Now imagine you are walking along a beautiful white sandy beach.
The sand is very soft so you take off your shoes and your socks.
You walk on the warm white sand.
You can feel the sun beneath your feet.
Can you feel it between your toes?
Can you feel it?
Can you feel the sand flick up against the back of your legs?
The beach is wide and long.

It stretches for miles ahead.
At the far end of the beach you can see what looks like a lovely wooden cabin.
You walk towards it to go and see it.
As you walk you hear the sounds of the waves.
You can hear the sounds of them coming up and onto the sand.
You can even smell the ocean spray.
That lovely smell you can only find at the beach.
The ocean is a deep brilliant blue color and it sparkles in the sunshine.
It's like the waves are dancing just for you.
You can hear the magnificent sounds of the ocean waves so much louder now.
You can still hear the waves coming onto the shore.
You can smell the clean salty water.
You can even smell the sand.
You look out at the ocean.
It is the deepest blue you have ever seen.
As you reach what you thought was a cabin, you realize it's actually a beautiful white villa.
It's so pretty.
It has lovely big glass windows with window boxes.
There are butterflies dancing all around the flowers.
It has a little wrap around porch with a big swinging chair filled with soft cushions.
It looks very inviting.

You decide you want to go inside and see what it's like.
You gently tap on the door but there is no answer.
You tap again.
Still no answer.
So, you decide to go inside anyway.

You enter into a big lovely room filled with huge cushions, kind of like beanbags.
They are so big and the room is so bright and inviting.
You realize that all of the cushions are in a big circle.
You walk over to have a look and you give a little gasp for what you see.
The reason the cushions are in a big circle is because the lovely little white wooden villa has a glass floor.
It is very thick glass.
The kind of glass that doesn't break when you walk on it.
You take a seat on one of the soft cushions and take a look through the glass floor below you.
This is amazing!
Wow!
You can see the ocean below you.
The beautiful turquoise ocean.
You can see the water gently moving backwards and forwards.

As it flows in and out like the waves.
You see beautiful tiny little fish swimming by all glistening with color.
The colors are amazing so vivid and bright.
You see bigger fish again with bright dazzling colors.

They take no notice of you whatsoever.
They are just happily swimming along doing fishy things you know they like to do.
You can an eel smoothly gliding by.
The most amazing thing about this eel it has a tiny red top hat.
It looks kind of cool too.
It's kind of mesmerizing looking through the glass.
You wonder what else is swimming down below you.
What other delights are in store in the beautiful blue ocean.

You decide to stay here for a while and just watch the ocean.
It is teeming with all kinds of life.
You can even see the ocean floor.
You can see little crabs scurrying along in the sand.
One of them suddenly stops and looks up at you.

It looks like he's kind of smiling at you.
Surely crabs don't smile, do they?
He lifts up one of his claws and gives you wave and suddenly he curries off again.
Oh my! A crab just waved at you!
You give a little laugh.
As you watch some more you notice how kind all of the little creatures are.
They are helping each other to do things.
One little fish is helping another little fish move a rock out of the way.
Then you see the eel with the red top hat, come along too help .
He uses his nose and he just pushes the rock.
They are all so kind to each other.
This is so much fun to watch.
You can hear the crashing of the lapping of the ocean waves in this beautiful tropical paradise.
It sounds so peaceful and it's so calming and restful being here in this white wooden villa.
You think to yourself you would like to stay here forever and ever and ever.
So, settle yourself down on your very big soft cushion, and for a few moments just enjoy watching the undersea world.

See what else you can see.
See if there are any mysterious creatures that maybe you've never seen before.
If you like you can imagine yourself being under the water with them.
You can imagine breathing underwater just like the fish do.
Or maybe you prefer just to watch and learn about life under the sea right where you are on your big soft beanbag.

You have seen some amazing things in the water below you.
I really really enjoyed being here, but you realized now that you're feeling a bit sleepy.
So, you snuggle down even deeper in your big soft cushion.
You can still see the creatures below you.
You can still hear the sound of the ocean waves as they gently begin to lull you into a deep sleep.
Your eyes begin to feel heavy.
You find that your eyelids are beginning to droop.

Oh your body feels so peaceful.
So relaxed.

So calm and so very very heavy now.
You love being here in this beautiful tropical paradise.
It's so wonderful.
Just before your eyes begin to close, you see once again the little crab scurrying past.
And again he stops and looks at you and gives you a wave with his claw and then scurries off again.
You smile at him and think how lucky you are.

How lucky you are to be in such a beautiful place.
How lucky you are to be able to see how life is under the ocean waves.
You have seen how peaceful they live.
They all do live so peacefully together.
You have seen how they all help each other.
How kind they are to each other.
You think that kindness is a very wonderful thing.
You decide that from now on, you are going to be kind to everyone.

You close your eyes and just listen to the sounds of the ocean.
You can feel your breathing as it begins to slow down.

You feel your chest is just rising and falling very gently.
You listen to the rhythm of the waves as they gently begin to lull you into a beautiful and restful sleep.

Just listen to the waves as you go deeper and deeper into a sleep.
Feeling so peaceful so calm.

So relaxed and when you wake up in the morning, you will feel so refreshed and so very very happy.
You can always visit the little white wooden villa any time you want.

Now imagine you are on the most beautiful beach in the world.
The glorious white sand.
You can see trees on this beach but they are further back.
There's no one else there.
Just you.
You take off your shoes and your socks.
You walk along the sand and it feels nice and warm.
You can feel the sand beneath your toes.

You look ahead and you see a small clump of trees like palm trees.
You see a few rocks.
You think to yourself; I think I'll just go and have a sit down and look.
Just look around.
What can you see?
You see an odd bird flying past.
You see a few beautiful white fluffy clouds in the sky.
You see the most beautiful deep blue ocean.
You can hear the sounds of the waves as they come gently to the shore.
As you get nearer to this little clump of trees with a few big rocks, you wonder where these rocks came from.
There are no other rocks on the beach at all.
Just beautiful white sand.
You reach the little bump of trees and you decide to sit on one of the big shiny rock.
It has a few little dents in it.
It has iridescent colors in it.
Blue, pinks and purples.
You think this is a pretty rock.
It feels very smooth and it's rather shiny for a rock.
You sit yourself down and you think it's nice and warm.
Is it moving?

Oh don't be silly. Of course it's not moving.
Then you hear a voice "Get off my back!"
You jump off the rock and think who said that.
You look down as this rock really does move this time.
A little head pops out with an orange hat.

You are absolutely flabbergasted!
Is this rock alive?
Hmm well actually no, it's not a rock.
It's actually a huge turtle
This turtle with the orange hat is looking directly at you.
You say "Oh I'm really sorry! I didn't mean to sit on you. I thought you were a rock!"
The turtle laughs and says, "Okay I'll let you off."
It's a female turtle.
She looks and says, "My name is Tessie. What's yours?"
So, you tell her your name.

You ask her why she's just sitting there just doing nothing.
She tells you with a little sad look on her face, "Well do you see these vines on this tree?"

You say, "Hmm yea, I didn't notice it before but yeah."

"Well I've got one of the feet stuck in it and I can't get out. I've tried to bit it but it won't come off."

"Oh dear," you say, "well I can help."

So you kneel down in the warm sand and you dig a little bit because a foot has gone into the sun completely.

You see that the vine has wrapped itself around her lovely little foot.

She really can't move.

Very gently you lift her foot and you unwrap the wine from it.

You actually look at her foot and she's got little tiny nails.

They're painted orange.

She has orange toenails just like her hat.

You smile to yourself because you think it looks rather pretty.

You untangle Tessie completely and she stretches her leg.

She says, "Oh that feels so much better. I can move again! Thank you so much for being so kind to me, even though you did sit on me."

You laugh a little and you think oh she's really nice.

Tessie looks as you and says, "Would you like to ride on my back? I'm big and strong because I really am a big turtle."

You say yes.
"Please come on," she says.
So, you climb on her back and she lifts herself up to a full height.
She really is quite bit.
She slowly starts moving because she can't go very fast.
After all she is a turtle.
You wobble a bit but you keep ahold of her shell.
It wobbles from side to side as she lumbers along the sand.
It's amazing this beautiful creature is letting you ride on her back.
Or is it because you were so kind to her?
You feel good because you are kind to her.
You know that it's always good to be kind.
Always.

Tessie the turtle reaches the water.
She starts to walk in it and it gets deeper.
You feel your feet dangling in the water.
She turns to you and she says, "Would you like to go for a swim with me? I'll keep you safe. I'll keep you safe on my back as long as you keep a tight hold."
You think yeah why not. I can do that.
So, Tessie moves further and deeper into the water.

Then she begins to swim and it is amazing.
You are sitting on the back of a turtle in the biggest and deepest blue ocean you've ever seen.
It's not as wobbly now because she's not lumbering on the beach.
It's like you are floating because you can't see her legs which are swimming really quickly underneath you, but you can't see that.
It's like you're floating on a giant rock.
A giant rock with a head with an orange hat.
The sun is shining and it is so lovely and warm.
As Tessie head further out, it is so beautiful.
So so beautiful.
The waves are gentle.

As she swims further out you look around.
You can see a very large ship in the distance.
So far away it looks tiny, but you know it's a really big ship.
You turn to look somewhere else and there's a smaller ship.
Or maybe it's just because it's even further away?
You don't really know.
Tessie keeps swimming and as she does, she begins to chat.
She tells you she is 104 years old.

Oh my goodness!

Does anyone ever live to be 104 years old?

You turn to look behind you and as you do, you realize you are very very far out at sea.

The shore that you were on, the lovely golden white beach, is so tiny now.

You're not afraid.

You're really enjoying this and you know Tessie will keep you safe.

You turn back as Tessie chatters away telling you about her life, about her family, how many children she's got.

Lots and lots of children.

You look ahead of you again and you see a whale.

This huge enormous whale.

You see its tail come out of the water and go back down with a big splash.

You think oh that's a bit big.

Oh maybe we shouldn't get to close to it.

Tessie says, "Its okay. That's my friend Bert the whale."

Such an odd name for a whale.

She swims closer and right up to Bert.

Bert's eye is probably about the size of my head!

You think wow Bert can talk too!

He says, "Hello Tessie. What are you doing today? Where are you going? Who's that on your back?"

"This is my friend who helped me by untangling my foot, so im giving this beautiful little human a ride on my back."

You really are a kind person.
Okay Tessie. I'm off. I've got things to do today.
With a great big splash she dives into the water and you get drenched, but you laugh.
You don't fall off Tessie's back.
The water goes everywhere.
You can even taste it.
It's salty.
You and Tessie just laugh and then Tessie asks, "Would you like to see to where I live."
Well yes, but do you live on the beach?
Tessie says, "Now I live beneath the water."
I can't do that!
She says, "Yes you can."
With a quick flip of one of her feet, she throws a kind of mask on you.
You have no idea where she got it from but she gives it to you.
"You should put that on your face and you'll be absolutely fine. You'll be able to breath no problem at all."
What that she dives completely under the water.

You barely have time to get your mask on.

As you look around you are amazing.
You are beneath the ocean and actually bright and lit down here.
There are fish swimming past.
Lots and lots of fish.
They all nod to Tessie as they go past.
All different colors and different varieties.
Striped ones, spotty ones, beautiful bright blue ones.
You have no idea what they're called.
Tessie continues to swim.
She goes down and down and down.
She does not do too deep though.
What you see coming towards you is a lot of coral.
Behind that coral is brightly colored coral.
It looks like a little cave.
Tessie takes you into that cave.
When you get inside, the cave it lit up with sparkling lights.
Sparkling shining crystals.
There are other turtles in there.
Lots of them in fact.

Tessie said, "This is my family and all these turtles are my children."

There are hundreds of them.

This is a very large cave.

For a few moments you can swim around with Tessie and meet Tessie's children.

You find out what they do.

You find out if they all live together or do they have their own caves?

Ask them.

Maybe when you've met all of Tessie's children you could see if there are other caves.

There are lots of other caves and maybe you could swim around the ocean with Tessie, meet her friends, meet other sea creatures.

Maybe you can find birds and that whale again.

You can do anything you like here.

You can do it all with Tessie.

She will show you exactly where she lives.

If you like you could call it a village.

Not a village as you know it but it's her village.

It's her town.

It's her city.

You can do anything you want.

You might even find out that maybe they've got a fun fair too.

Oh would that be nice?

Maybe you could have an ice cream cone.
You imagine having ice cream underwater.

Now it's time for Tessie to take you back.
You had a wonderful time meeting her family and her friends.
You make sure you're back on Tessie's back.
She begins to swim very quickly and in no time at all your back.
Tessie has arrived back on the sandy shore.
You climb off her back.
You wonder what you're going to do now.
You're feeling a bit sleepy now.
You had a very exciting day so Tessie says, "Tell you what. Let you and I have a little sleep under this clump of trees. If I snuggle down, you can lean up against me and pretend I'm your pillow."
You think to yourself that is a really good idea because your eyes are beginning to close.
You get more tired by the second.
Tessie lays herself down, tucks in her feet and all you can see is part of her little hat.
Her bright orange hat sticking out.
You stretch beside her and lay on your back.
On her enormous shell is actually quite comfortable.
You put your head back and close your eyes.

Tessie says, "Wow. What a lovely day we had together. I really enjoyed meeting you. I want to regard you as a my very very special friend. You've been so kind to me. You know if you ever come back here again, we can always go and visit my family and my friends."
You mumble to yourself that would be nice.
You're so sleepy now so so tired.
You know that when you wake up, you will be back in your very own bed.
In your very own little room with the most wonderful memories of Tessie, the very large turtle.
So now just sleep.
Just rest.
Goodnight.
Sleep tight.

Now imagine you are walking towards the ocean.
Walking through a beautiful tropical forest.
You can see the trees around you.
Very tall and elegant trees.
You can smell the fresh clean air.
You can even hear the sounds of all the different animals and birds in this forest.
Can you hear them?

You can hear the waves up ahead of you.
You can hear the sounds of them coming up.
You can even smell the ocean spray.
That lovely smell you can only find at the beach.
Can you smell it?
You continue to walk along your path coming close to the sea.
As you come to the edge of the trees you see a brilliant blue color of ocean ahead.
You can hear the magnificent sound of the ocean waves, so much louder now.
You walk out of the forest and onto a long stretch of glorious white sand.
The sun is very soft, so you take off your shoes and socks.
You walk through the hot white sand towards the water.
You can feel the sun beneath your feet.
Feel it between your toes.
Can you feel it?
The beach is very wide and very long.
It stretches for miles ahead.
You can hear the waves going into the shore.
You can smell the clean salt water.
You can even smell the sand.
You look again at the ocean and it's the deepest blue that you have ever seen.

Now imagine yourself walking towards the water over the fine hot sand.

You're feeling a bit hot and just a little sticky now too.

As you walk you can see the sparkles of the sunshine dance upon the water's surface like a million tiny stars all shining just for you.

It looks so beautiful.

A wave washes over the sun towards you.

You can feel it touch your toes before gently receding.

You step forwards and more waves wash over your feet.

It feels so cool and refreshing.

So calming on your feet.

You walk a bit further into the clear clean water.

You can see the white sand under the water.

You can feel it between your toes.

Can you feel it?

Squash your toes into the sand.

Wiggle them about in the water.

You can see a few small fish rapidly swim past you.

Flashes of color as they pass by.

The water is very pleasant.
Cool but not too cold.

You walk a bit further into the water.
You decide you want to take a gentle swim.

Just enjoy the ocean for a few minutes.
Allow yourself to float and drift around in the beautiful deep blue ocean.
Just float around with all the little fish and just relax.

Now you are feeling very calm and refreshed.
You're feeling very peaceful and very very relaxed.
You walk out of the water and back onto the beach.
Feeling again the soft sand beneath your feet and your toes.
You walk along the water's edge and you feel free of any worries you might have had.
They've all gone.
All of your problems have been washed away.
You only feel very calm and very peaceful and so so relaxed.

You turn around and see a comfortable lounge chair and towel just for you.

You go over and you sit or lie there on the chair.
You may decide to spread the towel in the sun and just relax on the chair.
Just relaxing and enjoying the sunshine.
Enjoying the cool gentle breeze upon your face.
The warmth of the sun on your skin.
The sounds of the waves making you feel ever so peaceful and ever so happy.

You just watch the waves as they ebb and flow backwards and forwards.
Backwards and forwards.
You feel calm.
So calm.
So relaxed and so very very peaceful.
You just sit there either for a little while longer.
Enjoying this lovely relaxation that's been made just for you.

Now it's time for you to return back to your normal life.

It's time to come back home.
Now imagine you're walking on the most glorious sandy beach.
It's very soft and very white.

You can hear the gentle sound of the waves as the roll on the sandy beach.
You can even smell the ocean spray.
That lovely smell you can only find at the beach.
The ocean is a brilliant deep blue color.
The sounds of the ocean waves is so much louder now.
You walk through the hot white sand towards the water.
You can feel the sand beneath your feet.
You can feel it between your toes.

The beach is very long and it stretches for miles ahead.
You go over and you step into the water and it covers your ankles.
It feels so cool and fresh on your skin.
There are large rocks and what seems to look like a cave further along the beach.
You think to yourself that maybe you'll explore it later.

For now you just keep paddling along.
You notice something in the ocean near those rocks.
You spot the head of a seal bobbing up and own.
It seems to be very near the cave you just noticed.
You decide to go over and take a look.
What you see is a tiny white seal.
It looks like it may be struggling.
You wonder what's wrong.
The tiny white seal looks like it's caught in something.

You call out to the little seal and you ask if it's okay.
A tiny little voice shouts, "Please help me!"
You rush over and you see that the little seal is caught in an old fishing line.
It's tangled around its flippers, so you go straight over and help that little seal break free.
The little seal gives you a great big grin.
"Thank you very much for your help."
The little seal tells you his name.
His name is heart.
Heart is a very tiny white seal.
He's so tiny he could fit into the palm of your hand.
He has the biggest blue eyes you have ever seen.
They are so bright and so kind.
Heart tells you that he loves going on adventures.

He loves going to swim lessons and on boat rides with his family.
He loves exploring places he's never been before.
Although, sometimes it gets him into trouble.
You see, his parents worry about him very much when he doesn't tell them where he's going, or even who he is with because they always go places together as a family.
They never go anywhere without each other.

Sometimes heart gets so excited about where he wants to go he forgets to tell them.
He just swims off.
Heart is the baby of the family so he really shouldn't be going anywhere on his own just yet.
Just now you hear voices calling.
It sounds like they're coming from the cave you wanted to explore, so you and Heart swim over there and take a look.
Heart recognizes the voices and it's his family.
It's his mom, his dad and his auntie.
They have been looking everywhere for Heart.
They swim over to you both with big smiles on their faces.
They are so relieved to have found Heart and that he's okay.

They have been worried sick looking for him.
They all chatter at once.
You can't really understand what they're saying.
They're all talking together but they are happy.
Heart introduces you to his family.
The biggest seal comes up to you and Heart says this is my dad Blobby.
Blobby is the biggest out of the family.
He has a beautiful gray color with majestic black.
Blobby is a super chunky seal and very round.
Next Heart introduces you to his mom.
Her name is Sweetie and she is smaller than Blobby.
She is a very beautiful white seal with lovely soft fluffy fur.
She has the sweetest black eyes and Heart looks very like his mom.

Finally Heart introduces you to his aunt.
Her name is Spot.
Spot is a spotted grey seal with kind and very wise yellow eyes.
She is the longest seal out of all of them.
Spot is Blobby's sister.
Heart tells them how you rescued him and how you untangled him from the net.
They can't thank you enough.

They are so happy.
As a reward they invite you to tour their house.
Blobby says, "Get on my back. It'll be much quicker."

You climb up on Blobby's back.
It's so comfortable and so soft, but you hang on tight.
Blobby says, "Okay we are all ready to go!"
Within seconds you are going at a great speed.
It's fantastic!
Water is splashing everywhere, and you absolutely love it.
The five of you ride off to Heart's home.

You enjoy the ride.

You arrive at their home and you are amazed.
It's actually a boat.
You thought that all seals lived under the ocean waves.
Well this family lives on an actual boat!

They live on a boat that bobs up and down in the sea.
How cool is that?

This isn't just any old boat though, this boat is shaped like a seal.
It is huge!
It even has a flag flying high on the top of the mast with a picture of a seal on it too.
It's very luxurious.
Wow! You have never seen anything like this before.
It's wonderful!
Sweetie goes into the kitchen saying that she's going to make a pot of tea now for the adults.
But for you and Heart there's freshly squeezed orange juice.
While you wait for Sweetie to make the tea, you have a little look around the room you are in.
There are family photos everywhere.
There is a bookcase overcrowded with books of all kinds.
They obviously all like to read here.
You even see one of your favorite stories on one of the shelves.
There is a really big log fire burning.
There are big squishy comfy chairs all around and even bigger squishier sofas.
There are lovely vases filled with flowers of all sorts of colors.
There even is a tropical fish tank full of brightly colored fish.

Heart says that they are his pets.
He loves fishes and they are his friends.
You feels so comfy and so warm here.
You think it would be great if you could live on a boat like this.
Heart asks you is you would like to see the rest of the boat.
He says he will show you his bedroom too.
You set off and have a good explore around his lovely home.
For a few moments you see what else there is to find.
How many rooms are there on this very big boat that looks like a seal?

Just have fun with Heart for a few moments while you wait for your tea.

You and Heart now return to the lovely comfy living room and meet up with Blobby, Sweetie and Spot.
They are all sitting around a small table with your drinks on it and the biggest and fattest chocolate cake you have ever seen.
Wow! That's a lot of chocolate!
Heart tells you that his mom made it.
She makes the best cakes in the whole wide world.

You take a bit out of your piece of the cake and wholeheartedly agree with him.
It is delicious and very chocolaty.
The five of you happily eat your chocolate cake and drink your drinks.

Heart gives you a great big yawn.
Then you do too.
Sweetie asks you if you would like a sleepover with Heart.
You say you can stay in his room with him and say "Oh yes please. That would be lovely."
Blobby and Spot say goodnight to both of you and Sweetie takes you and Heart ot his bedroom.
She tucks you both and says goodnight.
Then she switches off the lights.
It's then that an amazing thing happens.
There's a big round window in the ceiling of Heart's bedroom that you didn't notice before.
Through this window you can see the moon high up in the sky.
You can see lots and lots of stars all gently shining down on your beds.
It's like you have your own private show of dancing lights.
It's so beautiful.

You both watched the stars feeling so peaceful, so calm and so happy.
You begin to feel your eyes getting very heavy and a bit sleepy.

You can hear the gentle lapping of the waves, as they move against the side of the boat.
This makes you feel so safe.
You feel your eyes gently closing now as you take a deep breath in and let out a long happy sigh.
You have made a very special friend today who has a very special family too.
Remember you can come visit heart and his family anytime you want to.
You can visit Blobby, Sweetie and Spot too.
You take another deep breath in and slowly breathe out.
Feeling that your body has already gone to sleep, you gently close your eyes and drift into the most wonderful sleep.
Always remember you are safe.
You are loved and you are protected.
Always.

CHAPTER 4

Magical Forest Friends

Close your eyes and be very still.
Take a big deep breath in through your nose, and slowly and gently breathe out through your mouth.
Take another deep breath in and slowly and gently breathe out through your mouth.
One more time, big deep breathe in and slowly and gently breath out through your mouth.
Relax feeling peaceful and calm.
Now, imagine that you are surrounded by a beautiful white light.
This light surrounds your whole body and it's beneath your feet and above your head.
You are inside this light just like a caterpillar safe in its cocoon.
This light is very special and inside this light you know that you are always safe.

You know that you are always loved.
You know that you are always protected.

Now, imagine that you are outdoors walking in a lovely green forest.
The nighttime is approaching fast, but at the moment it's still light out.
The sun is beginning to set and the sky is starting to darken ever so slightly.
The air around you is still and calm.
You can hear all the different sounds as the creatures of the forest begin to settle for the night.
Can you hear them?
The birds are flying home to rest now.
The tiny animals are rushing to their homes.
Can you see the foxes calling out to each other as they come out for the night to begin their hunt, or food, or just to play with each and have some fun.
Can you hear the sounds of breaking twigs and the rustle of leaves as each tiny animal scurries to their warm safe home.
As you walk along, you hear a different sound coming from the treetops high above.
You're not sure what it is yet.
You listen harder and you realize that what you are hearing is the call of the night owl.

The sound of a very large owl indeed.
You walk a bit deeper into the lush forest as the sky gets darker still.
It feels so peaceful here, so calming and the night is quieter.
There are now no sounds of any animals as they are all tucked into their warm cuzy homes.
The birds are all asleep in their nests, but you hear the call of the night owl.
You hear the flapping of its large but gentle wings.
The sound gets closer to you when suddenly right before you plops down with big round glasses perched on the end of his nose.
Startled, you take a step back wondering what to do.
The large owl nods his head at you and says, "Good evening."
He pushes his glasses back upon his nose because they keep sliding down.
Your mouth drops open and you think to yourself did this owl just speak to me?
Well yes, he did.
Because you didn't answer the old owl clears his throat again with a big hmm and says again, "good evening."
You say it back to him with a smile.
The owl smiles back and tells you he is off for a fly around.

He says he spotted you from high above, when he thought to himself if you would like to fly with me. So he flew down to ask you.

He often asks little humans if they would like to fly with him.

He says that he gets rather lonely flying on his own. You are so excited by this that you say, "Oh yes please! Who wouldn't want to fly with an owl. I know I would!"

As you look around you notice that the sun has gone down and been replaced by a beautiful silver moon. It's actually quite dark now.

You can see all around you with the shining glow of the moonlight.

The old owl who is very larger than you tells you to grab hold of his feathers and pull yourself up onto hit back.

He tells you not to pull any of his feathers out though as it will hurt a lot.

You grab the old owl's feathers and heave yourself up onto his back being very careful.

He then tells you to hold on tight.

He begins to run flapping his huge wings.

The old owl runs and runs and runs but nothing seems to be happening.

Nothing seems to be happening, but the old owl still keeps running.

He's now starting to get a bit puffed and his huge wings keep flapping away.

You look ahead and you see that you are heading towards the edge of a cliff.

Oh no!

You're starting to get a bit worried now, as the cliff edge is getting very close.

The old owl hasn't even taken off yet but the old owl still keeps running.

He is still puffing away.

Then just as you get to the edge of the cliff the old owl jumps off.

Then the two of you swoop down going faster and faster.

The old owls wings are spread really wide and flapping away like crazy.

You close your eyes really tight and cling onto the owl's feathers.

Just as you think you're going to crash the old owl lifts himself higher and higher up into the night sky.

You slowly open your eyes and take a look around.

What you see takes your breath away.

You are high up in the sky gliding on the back of the owl.

The moon is shining brightly and the stars are twinkling like beautiful diamonds in the sky.

It's so still and quiet up here.

All you can hear is the gentle breeze as it washes over you.
The old owl is no longer flapping his wings.
He is gliding on the currents of air all around you.
He turns his body to the left and you look below you.
Far below you is a beautiful lake surrounded by your lovely forest.
You can see the reflection of the moon on the water's surface.
You can even see your own reflection on the back of the owl as he gets closer to the water.
For a few more moments you fly with this beautiful old owl.
You feel the gentle breeze on your face.
Talk to the owl and ask what his name.
You can ask him whatever you want.
Don't forget to tell him who you are as well.
For now just fly.

The beautiful old owl returns you to the ground of your forest.
You gently land and thank this beautiful creature for letting you fly with him.
You ask if it would be possible for you to do this again.
He says of course it is.

All you have to do is go for an evening walk in the forest look and he will be there.

The old owl flaps his huge wings, runs for a little bit and then takes off.

You watch him disappear up into the night sky.

You can hear him make the sound that only owls can make, as he slowly gets smaller and smaller.

You feel so happy and so content now.

So peaceful.

Now it's time to leave this beautiful place, leave the beautiful wise old owl.

You can come and visit him anytime you want.

Now you are back in your own bed.

As you gently rest take a deep breath and slowly breathe out.

Feel yourself becoming more and more relaxed.

One more time deep breath and gently breathe out more and more sleepy.

So peaceful.

Now, imagine that you are in a very lush green forest and the sun is shining.

It's a very beautiful day.

The sun is peeking through the leaves and the branches of the tall trees.

There are so many trees.

You feel very calm, very relaxed and very very peaceful.

You can hear birds singing to each other.
Can you hear them flying from tree to tree to have a little char with each other?
They sound so happy as they tweet away high up in the branches.
Can you hear the birds singing?
Can you hear them chatting to each other?
As you walk along you notice something ahead of you sitting against a very tall and bushy tree.
You are not sure what it is so you walk a bit quicker.
As you look and get closer to the tree, you realize it's a fox!
It's a rather beautiful fox with a very bushy red tail pointing straight up.
This fox is sitting cross legged at the base of the tree with his eyes closed.
He looks like he's meditating and you can hear the beautiful sound of the Tibetan singing bowl but you can not see one anywhere.

You can even smell incense burning a lovely sweet aroma.
It kind of tickles your nostrils.
You don't want to disturb the fox so you stop and stand still.

You just watch and notice that he has on very brightly colored trousers with lots of red, blues and even purple colors.

He is also wearing a very shiny silver waistcoat with really bright yellow buttons.

He looks like he's got tiny suns all over him.

He also has the biggest orange hat you have ever seen with a big pink feather sticking out form the top.

He is a colorful sight to see.

It's like he had no idea what to wear when he got dresses this morning so he put all of his cloths on.

He also has a very large metal framed glasses on.

Normally foxes are very shy and try to hide themselves away but this one clearly isn't.

As you stand there trying to be ever so quiet he opens his eyes and peers over the top of his glasses.

He gives you a great big smile and says, "Hello. How can I help you today?"

You tell him you were just out walking and came across him but did not want to disturb him so tried to be very quiet.

He smiles again and tells you to come and sit beside him so you do.

He tells you his name is Mr. Chi and he asks what your name is so you tell him.

Around Mr. Chi's neck is a mala bead necklace.

They are beads that help you when you meditate.
They are very beautiful.
Mr. Chi pulls another set of mala beads out of his pick and gives them to you as a gift.
He tells you to put them on.
You thank him for his lovely gift and you put on the necklace.
He asks if you would like to meditate with him and you say, "Oh yes! I'd like to do that!"
All he wants you to do is close your eyes and just breathe gently in and out, in and out.
So you do as he asks.

With your eyes closed you can hear the sound of the Tibetan singing bowl even more clearly now but you still can't see it.
You can smell the incense even stronger.
Can you smell it?
Can you smell how strong it is?
You realize that you can hear Mr. Chi speaking but he's not using his voice to speak you can hear his thoughts in your mind.
How clever Mr. Chi is with his voice.
In your mind he asks you again how can he help you so you sit and think for a moment and then you tell him.

You tell him whatever is on your mind and whatever may be worrying you.

So, for a few moments you just sit with Mr. Chi and tell him what is on your mind and he will give you the answer that you need to hear because Mr. Chi has all the answers to everything.

Mr. Chi can solve any problem because Mr. Chi is a very clever fox.

Mr. Chi now asks you to open your eyes and just breathe gently and slowly for a minute or so.

He asks you to come with him into his den for a nice cool drink and a biscuit so that you can have a chat.

You both get up and walk around to the back of the tree where there is a door which Mr. Chi opens and you both enter the lovely room.

The room is very comfortable and very colorful just like Mr. Chi.

There are beads hanging everywhere.

There are beads on the walls.

There are beads hanging over his cozy little lamps.

There are even beads hanging from the ceiling all in many different colors.

There is a nice warm flower glowing and there are flowers everywhere.
Mr. Chi likes flowers.
He tells you his favorite flowers are tulips and he asks you what your favorite flower is and you tell him.
Mr. Chi tells you to sit in his best chair which is a nice big concrete armchair with lots of colorful cushions on it.
There is color everywhere in Mr. Chi's home.

You sit down on his best chair and take the cool drink Mr. Chi offers you.
Beside the comfy chair is a little table and Mr. Chi puts down on it a plate of delicious biscuits.
For a few moments you just sit with Mr. Chi, the clever fox, and have a chat about anything you want.
Maybe you can ask Mr. Chi how is he cleverest fox in the kingdom.
You can ask him why everyone comes to him with their problems.
Maybe you can even ask him where on Earth did he get those crazy cloths from.
This is now your time with the clever fox so make the most of it as he a busy fox.

Whatever you feel like talking about Mr Chi will listen because today you are his favorite person.

Now it's time for you to say goodbye to Mr. Chi and thank him for letting you meditate and chat with him and for seeing those amazing clothes.

It's time for you to thank him for giving you a lovely cool drink and some of your favorite biscuits.

It's time for you to leave his lovely cozy den and to return to your lovely home.

Now, imagine that you are in a beautiful lush green jungle and this jungle has the most amazing trees.

Some of them are very tall.

So tall that they look as if they are almost touching the sky.

Some of them are a bit smaller and a bit fatter.

Some of them have very strange vines dangling from them.

You are deep in the jungle and you realize that you've been hearing lots of strange noises.

You're not really sure where they are coming from, but they don't scare you at all.

You can hear the sounds of birds as they fly from treetop to treetop.

There are several different birds calling out to each other and you can hear them.

You can also hear the breeze fluttering through the leaves on the tree tops.
Stop just for a second and close your eyes.
Enjoy the variety of all the different sounds all around you.

You can hear the sounds of a big jungle cat far off in the distance and you can hear him calling out to his family.
Maybe he's calling them home for supper.
Maybe he just wants to know where they are.
You can even hear the sound of monkeys chattering to each other.
Can you hear them?
Some of them are quite loud.
You wonder what they are saying to each other.

If you listen really hard, you might be able to understand what they are saying.
Take a moment and listen to them.

You continue to walk through this lovely lush green jungle but you've never noticed before just how many shades of green there are.
Its beautiful.

The light in the forest cascades down through the leaves like twinkling lights.
There are plants and moss everywhere.
You can hear the many tiny animals of the jungle all moving out of the way running fast hoping you can't see them.
They are too quick for you.
You notice that the sun is starting to dip.
There is a lovely orange red glow in the sky.
You can see the colors of the sky peeking through the top of the trees.
As you continue your walk you come across an old fallen tree just lying on the ground.
You decide to have a little sit and rest your legs.
As you sit there, you can hear movement behind you.
You turn to have a look your mouth drops open in a gasp.
You are amazed because standing in front of you is a chimpanzee.
A chimpanzee with a bright red bowtie around his neck and a bright red hat sitting on top of his head.
The chimpanzee tips his hat to you and says good afternoon.
Did this chimpanzee really just say good afternoon?
Before you can reply, he sits himself down next to you and makes himself comfortable.

He takes off his hat and lays it gently on the fallen tree.
He gives you a very big grin.
He tells you that his is gathering friends for his afternoon tea.
He asks if you would like to come too.
You would love to come and how lovely would that be.
The chimpanzee puts his red hat back on and stands up.
He says, "Okay then follow me!"
The two of you set off together.
You go off and gather the rest of the chimpanzee's friends.
After a little while, you come across a very big tiger with a very large head.
He is also wearing a bow tie but blue.
He also has a big cowboy hat.
He grins at you and you notice he has very large teeth.
He is not scary at all, in fact, he is a bid old softie.
The three of you keep on moving.
You keep on moving along just looking around.
You come across to a clearing of the jungle.
In the middle of the clearing there is a table and five chairs.

Sitting at the table is a very large elephant with a with bow tie around his neck and a large floppy white hat.

Next to him is a snake who also has a pink bow tie to match hit pink hat.

The chimpanzee and the tiger walk over and sit down.

The beckon you to sit down on the remaining chair.

You look down at the table and see a big flowery teapot with five China cups and saucers.

There is a sugar bowl and fresh cup of milk.

There are scones with strawberry jam and fresh whipped cream.

There is a huge plate of cookies of various sizes and shapes.

There is also a large chocolate cake sitting in the center of the table with flakes of chocolate all around it.

There is also a plate of peanut butter sandwiches for everyone.

There is a massive pitcher filled with lemonade for anyone who would not want to drink tea.

There is a bowl filled to the top of fresh apples, bananas, pears, oranges, peaches and many other different kinds of fruits.

It is like a big feast!

Everything looks so delicious and a good thing you're hungry!

The chimpanzee realizes that no one has told you their names.
So, he introduces himself and his friends.
He tells you that his name is Chico Chico the chimpanzee, his friends are Tommy the tiger, Eddie the elephant and Sid the snake.
He asks you what your name is so you tell him.
You ask them why they are all wearing bowties and hats.
Sid says because they always get dressed up for afternoon tea.
It wouldn't be proper if they didn't.
For a little while you just sit with your new friends and enjoy your feast.
Ask them all the questions that are bouncing around in your head.
Ask them where they all live, who they live with and anything else you want to ask.
They are so thrilled that you are having afternoon tea with them.
They say they don't have important guests very often.

Now, is your chance to ask all the things you wanted to about the lives of chimpanzees, tigers, elephants and snakes.

Now, it's time for the tea party to end.
Everyone has to go home now, and you have to go home too.
So, you stand up and thank these beautiful animals for inviting you to their Tea Party.
Thank them all for the lovely food, but most of all thank them for telling you all about their lives in this huge lush green jungle.
Chico the chimpanzee hands you a little box with a silver ribbon tied around it.
He tells you that it is a gift for you.
You thank him very much for the wonderful gift.
He tells you that if you ever want to come to the tea party again all you have to do is come to the lush green jungle and he will find you.
You smile and you wave goodbye to your new friends and start to walk away.

Now, imagine that you are in a beautiful lush green rainforest.
This forest has the most amazing trees and some of them are very tall indeed.

So tall in fact that they look as if they are touching the sky.

There are so many luscious green trees here.

You can hear all kinds of sounds coming from the forest.

You can hear lots of different birds.

You can hear the sounds of animals moving around.

You can even hear sounds of water running over rocks.

You can't see it, but you can hear it.

It is very relaxing.

You find yourself walking along a path that winds in and out on the forest floor.

You are just enjoying yourself in this beautiful rainforest minding your own business when suddenly you hear the sounds of snoring, loud thunderous snoring.

My goodness!

You follow the sound until it leads you to a tree that looks very interesting.

You step in front of it and take a good look where the snoring is coming from.

The snoring is so loud now that you have to cover your ears.

You are wondering what on earth is making that sound.

They must be very deep asleep.

This particular tree looks like a secret tree house.
There is a sign carved into the tree saying, "Berry Norma Residence."
You wonder what on earth is Berry and Norman.
The snoring suddenly stops, and you hear movement coming from above.
You look upwards trying to see what is moving around up there.
Your eyes adjust and then to your surprise you see a sloth!
Its tail is wound around the branches and is hanging upside down looking at you with very big sleepy eyes.
They move extremely slowly, and they love being high up in the treetops.
To your surprise the sloth speaks to you and says, "Hello!"
It's a girl sloth and tells you her name is Amazing.
Amazing has a bright yellow hat with a big green feather in it.
It makes her look as if sunshine is coming out from the top of her head.
You say hello back to Amazing and you tell her your name.
She asks if you would like to come up and meet her family and see where she lives.
You say, "Of course!"

Amazing drops down a rope ladder for you and you climb up.

You would love to live high up in the treetops like her.
When you reach the first level there is a spiral staircase and it's wrapped around the whole tree.
When you get to the top of the staircase you stand next to amazing.
She adjusts her big yellow hat and says, "Follow me."
Amazing takes you to her front door and you see that her house is a wooden circular lodge.
Her home is made purely for snooze, relaxation and sleep.
There are big soft fluffy cushions everywhere.
There is also a speaker system playing sweet relaxation music.
You really like Amazing's home.
Amazing introduces you to her dad Barry.
You notice he has an earring on his left ear and a baseball cap on his head.
Her mom is called Norma and he only has one slipper one because she doesn't know where the other one is.
Cyril is her brother who is Amazing's older brother.

He is a grumpy teenager who keeps picking his nose.
Amazing seems to be the only normal one in her family.
This family has the best music and they love playing it very loudly.
You take a walk over to the window and take a look outside.
You can see the beautiful panoramic view above the treetops of the rainforest.
You notice this lovely family of sloths have a speaker system scattered all around the forest.
When you turn around everything is like in slow motion.
They even speak in slow motion.
Norma gives you a nice cup of tea and you all sit down and have a little chat.
You tell them all about your family, where you live, what your favorite things are and who your best friend is.
For a few moments sit and chat with this amazing family of sloths.
Find out about them too and don't forget to drink your cup of tea!

When you finished your tea, Barry says, "its now time for sleep."

He asks you if you would like to stay and have a little nap too.
Of course you say yes!
They have been up for two already and they are exhausted.
It's nice to have a chat with new friends.
Sloths like to get at least 18 hours of sleep because their world is so very slow.
You realize that outside of this amazing home, there is light rain falling.
It's making you feel very sleep listening to it.
You go outside and you choose a very comfy chair.
It's a comfy chair indeed.
It has a big soft pillow for your head.

You take a seat and you can hear the soft gentle music playing through their amazing speaker system.
It's making you feel very drowsy.
It makes you feel so sleepy.
So sleepy that you finally find it hard to open your eyes.
That's okay because you don't have to open your eyes if you don't want to.
All you have to do is relax.

You're in the chair with a big soft pillow listening to the rain as it helps you to fall gently to sleep.

Can you hear the soft and wonderful sounds of the beautiful music?

You are drifting deeper and deeper into the most wonderful night's sleep ever.

So snuggle down.

You feel so safe and so protected.

So very loved.

When you wake up in the morning you will feel completely refreshed, bright, alert and ready to begin the new amazing day ahead.

Each night from now on, you will sleep better and better.

Deeper and deeper.

Night night.

Sleep tight.

CHAPTER 5

Positive Bedtime Affirmations

Welcome to your happiness and imagination affirmations.

This is where we will focus only of the good feelings when we talk to ourselves in a positive way.

We feel good and great when amazing things happen in our lives.

Listen to these positive affirmations and repeat them in your head or out loud.

Great things flow to me.

I am a great listener.

People listen to me.

I am blessed.

The world needs me.

I have a brilliant brain.

I am growing up to be happy and healthy.

Everything always goes well for me.

I am generous.
I am helpful.
I am kind to others, and I am kind to myself.
I have so many people that love me.
Sharing is caring.
I can use my imagination to create great things.
I sleep deeply every night.
I believe I am great.
I tell the truth.
I speak kind words.
I share my feelings.
My feelings are important.
I make good choices.
I feel warm and fuzzy on the inside.
Healthy food makes my body feel good.
I stand up tall and I sit up straight.
I am proud of who I am.
I am full of amazing ideas.
I feel grateful for all the fun things and people in the world.
I love our beautiful planet Earth.
I love the trees, the clouds, the Sun and the breeze.
The trees, birds, and animals are my friends.
I love all of the wonderful animals on Earth.
I love sharing our planet with so many interesting people.
I sleep deeply every night like I'm on a fluffy cloud.

I can make my dreams come true.
I can choose to feel happy at any time.
I am free.
I am made of stardust.
I am a star.
I shine bright every day.
When I ask for help, I always get the help I need.
I have a super day every day.
I respect others and others respect me.
It feels good to use my manners.
When other people make mistakes I forgive them quickly.
When I make mistakes I forgive myself quickly.
Just like the clouds clear when it stops raining, bad times don't last forever. The Sun always shines brighter.
I feel calm and peaceful.
I can be whatever I want to be.
I love dreaming big with my imagination.
I love my body, my hair, my skin, my eyes and my nose.
I am perfect as I am.
I love being me.
Smiling makes me feel happy.
I am always super healthy.
I have everything I need.
I am always safe.

I always do my best.
I believe in myself.
I am loved.
I am smart.
I feel so happy like it's my birthday every day.
I am brave.
I can do anything.
I think positive thoughts.
My mind is powerful.
I sleep deeply every night.
I am so kind to others and I am kind to myself.
I have so many people that love me.
I love my friends and my friends love me.
I can create anything.
I am a creative genius.
I am the painter of my life.
What I feel is important.
I love having fun.
There is always more fun ahead.
I say thank you for all the wonderful things in my life.
Thank you.
Thank you.
Thank you.
I say thank you for all the exciting things in my future.
Thank you.
Thank you.

Thank you.
I am perfect as I am.
I'm a supper happy super kid.
I play well with others.
I am very special.
I am unique.
There is only one of me in the whole world.
I have so much exciting energy.
I love learning new things.
I'm a fast learner.
I am more than enough just as I am.
I am important.
I am worth of all great things.
I deserve all great things.
I sleep deeply every night.
Great things flow to me.
I'm a great listener.
People listen to me.
I am blessed.
The world needs me.
I have a brilliant brain.
I am growing up to be happy and healthy.
Everything always goes so well for me.
I am generous.
I am helpful.
I am kind to others and I am kind to myself.
I have so many people that love me.

Sharing is caring.
I can use my imagination to create great things.
I sleep deeply every night.
I believe I am great.
I tell the truth.
I speak kind words.
I make good choices.
I feel warm and fuzzy on the inside.
Healthy food makes my body feel good.
I stand up tall and I sit up straight.
I am proud of who I am.
I am full of amazing ideas.
I feel grateful for all the fun things and people in the world.
I love our beautiful planet Earth.
I love the trees, the clouds, the sun and the breeze.
The trees, birds and animals are my friends.
I love all the wonderful animals on Earth.
I love sharing our planet with so many interesting people.
I sleep deeply every night like I'm on a fluffy cloud.
I can make my dreams come true.
I can choose to be happy at any time.
I am free.
I am made of stardust.
I am a star.
I shine bright every day.

When I ask for help, I always get the help I need.
I have a super day every day.
I respect others and others respect me.
It feels good to use my manners.
When other people make mistakes I forgive them quickly.
When I make mistakes I forgive myself quickly.
Just like the clouds clear when it stops raining, bad times don't last forever. The Sun always shines brighter.
I feel calm and peaceful.
I can be whatever I want to be.
I love dreaming big with my imagination.
I love my body, my hair, my skin, my eyes and my nose.
I am perfect as I am.
I love being me.
Smiling makes me feel happy.
I am always super healthy.
I have everything I need.
I am always safe.
I always do my best.
I believe in myself.
I am loved.
I am smart.
I feel so happy like it's my birthday every day.
I am brave.

I can do anything.
I think positive thoughts.
My mind is powerful.
I sleep deeply every night.
I am so kind to others and I am kind to myself.
I have so many people that love me.
I love my friends and my friends love me.
I can create anything.
I am a creative genius.
I am the painter of my life.
What I feel is important.
I love having fun.
There is always more fun ahead.
I say thank you for all the wonderful things in my life.
Thank you.
Thank you.
Thank you.
I say thank you for all the exciting things in my future.
Thank you.
Thank you.
Thank you.
I am perfect as I am.
I'm a supper happy super kid.
I play well with others.
I am very special.
I am unique.

There is only one of me in the whole world.
I have so much exciting energy.
I love learning new things.
I'm a fast learner.
I am more than enough just as I am.
I am important.
I am worth of all great things.
I deserve all great things.
I sleep deeply every night.
Great things flow to me.
I'm a great listener.
People listen to me.
I am blessed.
The world needs me.
I have a brilliant brain.
I am growing up to be happy and healthy.
Everything always goes so well for me.
I am generous.
I am helpful.
I am kind to others and I am kind to myself.
I have so many people that love me.
Sharing is caring.
I can use my imagination to create great things.
I sleep deeply every night.
I believe I am great.
I tell the truth.
I speak kind words.

I make good choices.
I feel warm and fuzzy on the inside.
Healthy food makes my body feel good.
I stand up tall and I sit up straight.
I am proud of who I am.
I am full of amazing ideas.
I feel grateful for all the fun things and people in the world.
I love our beautiful planet Earth.
I love the trees, the clouds, the sun and the breeze.
The trees, birds and animals are my friends.
I love all the wonderful animals on Earth.
I love sharing our planet with so many interesting people.
I sleep deeply every night like I'm on a fluffy cloud.
I can make my dreams come true.
I can choose to be happy at any time.
I am free.
I am made of stardust.
I am a star.
I shine bright every day.
When I ask for help, I always get the help I need.
I have a super day every day.
I respect others and others respect me.
It feels good to use my manners.
When other people make mistakes I forgive them quickly.

When I make mistakes I forgive myself quickly.
Just like the clouds clear when it stops raining, bad times don't last forever. The Sun always shines brighter.
I feel calm and peaceful.
I can be whatever I want to be.
I love dreaming big with my imagination.
I love my body, my hair, my skin, my eyes and my nose.
I am perfect as I am.
I love being me.
Smiling makes me feel happy.
I am always super healthy.
I have everything I need.
I am always safe.
I always do my best.
I believe in myself.
I am loved.
I am smart.
I feel so happy like it's my birthday every day.
I am brave.
I can do anything.
I think positive thoughts.
My mind is powerful.
I sleep deeply every night.
I am so kind to others and I am kind to myself.
I have so many people that love me.

I love my friends and my friends love me.
I can create anything.
I am a creative genius.
I am the painter of my life.
What I feel is important.
I love having fun.
There is always more fun ahead.
I say thank you for all the wonderful things in my life.
Thank you.
Thank you.
Thank you.
I say thank you for all the exciting things in my future.
Thank you.
Thank you.
Thank you.
I am perfect as I am.
I'm a supper happy super kid.
I play well with others.
I am very special.
I am unique.
There is only one of me in the whole world.
I have so much exciting energy.
I love learning new things.
I'm a fast learner.
I am more than enough just as I am.
I am important.

Sleepy Willow

I am worth of all great things.
I deserve all great things.
I sleep deeply every night.

CONCLUSION

Thank you so much for reading *Bedtime Meditations For Kids Book 1*.

I hope this book has heled you have lots of wonderful dreams and amazing nights of sleep.

If you ever find yourself stressed out, angry, overwhelmed or sad you can always refer to the teachings of this book and re read it again.

If you enjoyed this book and if it has helped you have a better night's sleep, be sure to leave a thoughtful review on Amazon of how this book has helped you. This is so more kids like you can have amazing sleeps every night!

Thank you again for reading this book and I wish you all the love, happiness and amazing nights of sleep ahead!

www.ingramcontent.com/pod-product-compliance
Lightning Source LLC
Chambersburg PA
CBHW062034120526
44592CB00036B/2093